Evangelical belief

A short introduction to Christian
Doctrine in explanation of the
Doctrinal Basis of the Inter-Varsity
Fellowship

D1744116

Inter-Varsity Press

© Inter-Varsity Press, London

Inter-Varsity Fellowship
39 Bedford Square, London WC1B 3EY

First Edition October, 1935
Second Edition March, 1951
Third Edition April, 1961
Fourth Edition September, 1973

ISBN 0 85110 223 9

Printed in England by
Green & Co. (Lowestoft) Ltd., Crown Street, Lowestoft.

Contents

1 Introduction

Our Lord and the apostles laid down clearly the fundamentals of the Christian faith and life. Indeed we may define as fundamental those things which they made unmistakably clear, and we can conclude that other aspects of Christian teaching, however important in the particular situation of the church at any one time, are not of the same kind of basic importance. Furthermore, every human society and joint activity needs some common convictions and values. As church history amply illustrates, the Christian church is no exception to this rule. It has been held together and been spiritually strong when it has been united in the apostles' doctrine. But whenever other things have become more important than biblical truth, it has rapidly degenerated.

The writers of the New Testament repeatedly stressed that a careful and tenacious adherence to the original teaching of the Lord, and of those whom He had instructed, is the only way of remaining true to God. They anticipated that carelessness and confusion of thought would set in. They foresaw some of the most common and insidious errors and warned and forearmed the disciples accordingly. Timothy, for instance, was explicitly instructed to 'continue' in what he had learned from the apostles, 'to guard the deposit' (of truth) and to commit it to the keeping of 'faithful men who will be able to teach others also'. The New Testament affirms that the gospel-teaching, which we are required to believe, has been given 'once for all' and that we are earnestly to contend for that faith (Jude 3).

Because the church is so deeply divided on matters of doctrine, there are some, even among Christian leaders, who suggest that it is better to have very vague doctrinal statements, or even none at all. Such a view, however, fails to take into account two facts. In the first place, there is considerably greater agreement among the main branches of the Christian church than is commonly realized. For example, there has been virtual unanimity throughout the history of the church concerning such doctrines as are included in the Apostles' Creed.

Secondly, there is a tendency on the part of some to confuse the great affirmations of Christian doctrine themselves with the details of their application and their outworking in the day-to-day experience of Christians. The former are principles which can be stated with certainty and clarity, although their particular applications in experience offer scope for variety of opinion. The applications also depend to some extent on the nature of the immediate problems. Yet, in most cases, where such a variety of opinion exists, it presupposes an agreed 'body' of underlying principles. As the seventeenth-century preacher, Jeremy Taylor, once commented, 'I would that men would not make more necessities than God made, which indeed are not many.' Where, however, such necessary truths have been revealed by God they are not to be modified, weakened or superseded. There is a body of revealed truth in which the Christian's personal faith may rest and which constitutes his intellectual and spiritual anchorage.

Summaries of the most important aspects of Christian truth appear to have been in circulation from an early period in the Christian era. The best known examples are the Apostles' Creed (which summarizes the teaching of the apostles) and the Nicene Creed. After the Protestant Reformation in the sixteenth century, the doctrinal statements which have come to have the greatest influence among Protestants in the English-speaking countries are the Thirty-nine Articles of the Church of

England (1571) and their revision and amplification in the Westminster Confession of Faith (1647). The latter was designed to unite the Churches of England and Scotland, and has remained the 'subordinate standard' of the Church of Scotland and the majority of the other Presbyterian churches. The declarations of the early Congregational churches (Cambridge, 1648 and Savoy, 1680) are to a large extent revisions of the Westminster Confession. The first Methodist churches officially retained the Thirty-nine Articles of the Church of England as their doctrinal standard and prescribed for their ordinands a study of 'the Forty-four Sermons' of John Wesley, and his 'Notes on the New Testament'. Until recent years, the Minutes of the Methodist Conference annually reproduced their Founder's challenging 'Rules for a Helper' (*i.e.* a Lay Preacher).

The seventeenth-century Baptist churches modified the Westminster Confession and the Savoy Declaration to harmonize with their distinctive outlook. This process culminated in the Particular Baptist Confession of 1689. Later, towards the end of the nineteenth century, the Baptist Union adopted a shorter statement of doctrinal beliefs. In the case of a number of independent Baptist churches and assemblies of Brethren, apart from the local trust deeds of some congregations, the majority have adopted no detailed doctrinal statement, but accept as sufficient a reference to the teaching of the Bible as a whole.

It must at once be emphasized that all Protestant churches regard the teaching of such doctrinal statements as 'subordinate' to the Bible, which itself remains the supreme authority. From it all other doctrinal statements stand in need of proof. The affirmations of the Christian faith have to do with the Being of God and eternal truths which are beyond man's un-aided comprehension. The human mind can begin to appreciate them only when and where God has been pleased to take the initiative and to reveal Himself. This He has done (i) primarily in the Lord Jesus Christ, to whose Person and work the Holy Spirit bears witness in and through the Holy Scriptures;[1] (ii) in the Scriptures, to the authenticity of which both Christ and the Holy Spirit bear witness;[2] and (iii) through the Holy Spirit, who affirms by His witness that Christ is the divinely appointed Prophet, Priest and King. He also imparts to the believer the conviction that the Scriptures are the Word of God.[3]

The Christian has the responsibility and privilege of studying this Word, this revelation which God has given. It is the source of the special information with which he must occupy himself in seeking out those truths which are collectively referred to as 'the Faith'. Yet the contents of the Bible are far from being set out in the manner of a text-book of theology, and 'the Faith' is not there offered to us in a form which follows our usual scientific classifications. Doctrine is given as much by example as by definition. Consequently, the seeker after truth must follow the Bible's own method of approach and with all humility allow himself to be taught by the Holy Spirit.

It is not intended, however, to imply in these pages that a complete Christian theology is necessary for personal relationship with God. The New Testament clearly explains that there is only one indispensable way in which a man may approach God. He must confess himself to be a sinner who is both guilty and

[1] Heb. 1: 1, 2; 1 Tim. 2: 5; Jn. 16: 15; 17: 6; Heb. 12: 2.
[2] Rom. 15: 4; 2 Tim. 3: 16; 2 Pet. 1: 19.
[3] Jn. 16: 13, 14; 1 Cor. 2: 9-13; 1 Jn. 2: 20, 27.

helpless. He must sincerely repent of his sin, and believe on Jesus Christ as Saviour, Lord and God. But no-one can enjoy to the full the blessings of God's providence and grace, nor worthily fulfil his stewardship and responsibilities in God's church, unless he is adequately instructed in the essentials of divinely revealed truth. This he can become only by devoted study of God's written Word and by prayerful dependence upon the illuminating Spirit.

In such study it is essential to pay attention to the whole of the Bible, *i.e.* to the entire body of revealed truth, and to beware of the danger of seeing and insisting upon only certain aspects of the many-sided truth of God. In practice this means that it is necessary to summarize from the Bible those doctrines which are most characteristic of it and vital for an enlightened and vigorous faith. Among them, it is submitted, those which are included in the Doctrinal Basis of the Inter-Varsity Fellowship of Evangelical Unions must have a place. The Basis reads as follows:

The doctrinal basis of the Fellowship shall be the fundamental truths of Christianity, as revealed in Holy Scripture, including:—

a The unity of the Father, the Son and the Holy Spirit in the Godhead.

b The sovereignty of God in creation, revelation, redemption and final judgment.

c The divine inspiration and infallibility of Holy Scripture, as originally given, and its supreme authority in all matters of faith and conduct.

d The universal sinfulness and guilt of human nature since the fall, rendering man subject to God's wrath and condemnation.

e Redemption from the guilt, penalty and power of

sin *only* through the sacrificial death (as our Representative and Substitute) of Jesus Christ, the Incarnate Son of God.

f The resurrection of Jesus Christ from the dead.

g The necessity of the work of the Holy Spirit to make the death of Christ effective to the individual sinner, granting him repentance toward God and faith in Jesus Christ.

h The indwelling and work of the Holy Spirit in the believer.

i The one holy universal Church, which is the Body of Christ, and to which all true believers belong.

j The expectation of the personal return of the Lord Jesus Christ.

The committee members and officers of the Fellowship, who are required by the Constitution to sign the Basis, are invited to accept these statements in their plain sense, and to test them by Holy Scripture. It is to be noted that acceptance of the full Doctrinal Basis is required only from those in these two categories. Membership in the Christian Unions is open to anyone who affirms his faith in 'Jesus Christ as my Saviour, my Lord and my God' or — since there are certain local differences of expression — such other short declarations of faith as are in use. This procedure is in keeping with the practice of most denominations which look for a clear profession of faith in Christ from those seeking membership, but require considerably greater doctrinal undertakings from Christian ministers and other persons who are responsible for leadership.

The interpretations and explanations given in this booklet are not offered as detailed or binding judgments. The writers' concern is rather to enable the reader to appreciate more clearly how the IVF Doctrinal Basis is generally understood by those who subscribe to it. It is of greater importance that every Christian should seek by his own study to gain an improved understanding of what he believes and why he believes it. It is expected that office-bearers, in addition to the doctrines set out in these ten clauses, will accept and teach all else that can plainly be proved from Holy Scripture to have been part of the apostolic teaching. Further, it is hoped that this brief introduction will serve the larger purpose of encouraging all who read it to search further into Christian doctrine. To guide them in this, a short Bibliography has been included on pages 61-63.

A final comment needs to be made. A study of doctrine is not in itself enough. The gospel calls us to a form of life which should accompany our doctrine and, indeed, should arise out of it. The apostle Peter asks, in view of all these things, 'What sort of persons ought you to be in lives of holiness and godliness?'[4], while Paul urges Timothy: 'Do your best to present yourself to God as one approved, a workman who has no need to be ashamed, rightly handling the word of truth.'[5]

[4] 2 Pet. 3: 11.   [5] 2 Tim. 2: 15.

2 God and His Word

The introductory clause to the IVF Basis governs the whole. It reads: 'The doctrinal basis of the Fellowship shall be the fundamental truths of Christianity, as revealed in Holy Scripture, including:' The ten particular sections which then follow are intended to emphasize those points to which the Bible itself attaches primary importance. This clause also emphasizes that it is from one source — Holy Scripture — that all subsequent statements of the Basis have been derived. Only by divine revelation do we know such truths as those concerning the Being of God, the all-comprehending scope of His providence and rule and, also, the nature of His redeeming love to man. The following paragraphs discuss these crucial matters.

The Holy Trinity

The unity of the Father, the Son and the Holy Spirit in the Godhead.[1]

It is difficult accurately to maintain the balance of truth concerning the three Persons in the one Godhead.[2] The early disciples of our Lord were Jews and therefore strict monotheists. Yet they did not hesitate to acknowledge that Jesus was God the Son.[3] Further, the Lord Jesus Himself promised that He would send to them 'another Comforter', whom He also called 'the Spirit of truth'. He further explained that the Holy Spirit would have a special activity in the world as a result of His ascension.[4] In such ways, our Lord revealed a 'Tri-unity' in the Godhead.

---

[1] In the following sections the sentences at the head of each, in italics, are take consecutively from the Doctrinal Basis of the IVF Constitution (1960).
[2] 1 Jn. 5: 7; Mt. 3: 16, 17; 28: 19; 2 Cor. 13: 14.
[3] Jn. 20: 28.   [4] Jn. 16: 7-15.

Yet this revelation of a sacred Trinity is not inconsistent with the earlier monotheistic emphasis of the Old Testament. For, while the basic scriptural revelation is unmistakably clear that there is only one true God, this does not preclude the possibility that there may be real distinctions within the Godhead. Not only did the disciples assert that Jesus was God, but Christ Himself proclaimed His unity with God, and God the Father proclaimed Him as His 'only begotten Son'. The Christian today bears witness to this truth. He accepts the Old Testament's strong emphasis upon the fact of *one* sovereign God, and yet he sees that the New Testament has revealed a deeper significance and plurality of Persons in the Godhead. He therefore interprets the Old Testament in the light of the New, which joins Father, Son and Holy Spirit in the unity of the one true Godhead. The Father is not the Son. The Son is not the Holy Spirit. But the Father, the Son and the Spirit are equally God. As the creeds express it, they are one in 'substance' or 'essence'. Yet the Bible[5] clearly teaches, not only that the Son is a Person distinct from the Father, but that the Spirit is also distinct. He is described as 'the Spirit of God', 'the Holy Spirit of God', 'the Holy Spirit whom you have from God', 'the Spirit of his Son', and 'the Spirit of Christ'. The description of His coming, His relation to Christian believers and His work all imply the characteristics of a differentiated 'Person', who also acts in full harmony with the other Persons in the Trinity, and is equally God.[6]

[5] In the New Testament, Mt. 16: 15-17; 28: 19; Jn. 14: 16; 16: 7-15; 20: 24-31; 2 Cor. 13: 14; Eph. 2: 18; 1 Pet. 1: 2; Rev. 1: 4, 5.
[6] The Anglican Book of Common Prayer chooses John 3 as the Gospel for Trinity Sunday, presumably because it speaks of

A study of the names used for God and of references to Him throughout the Old and New Testaments[7] is very rewarding and throws light upon other parts of Scripture. A true view of the character of God is the foundation of all theology.[8]

Sovereignty

The sovereignty of God in creation, revelation, redemption and final judgment.

Right reverence for God, or what in the older phraseology is called 'the fear of the Lord', is 'the beginning of wisdom'.[9] Man can get his bearings, and come to a true understanding of himself, only as he acknowledges God as the Beginning and End of all existence.[1] He is to be acknowledged as the first and final Cause of all that is.[2] He reigns supreme.[3] Everything is within His will. He overrules the works of man and causes even man's wrath to praise Him.[4] All things were created by His decision and through His action.[5] All things are preserved by His power.

all three Persons doing things on behalf of men and because all that They do can be attributed only to God.

[7] For the unity of God, see Dt. 4: 35; 6: 4; Is. 42: 8; 44: 6. For the plurality of Persons, notice the use of 'us' in Gn. 1: 26; 3: 22; see Is. 6: 8 and references to the 'Spirit of God' and the Holy Spirit, *e.g*, Ps. 51: 11. God's Names in the Old Testament are more accurately studied from the Hebrew Text, but numerous aids are available for those who are unfamiliar with the languages of the Bible which will make the main points clear. For text-books of theology see the Bibliography, pp. 61, 62.

[8] Is. 6: 3; Jn. 4: 24; 1 Tim. 1: 17.

[9] Ps. 111: 10; Pr. 9: 10.

[1] Rom. 1: 21; Rev. 1: 8.

[2] Rom. 11: 36.

[3] Ps. 115: 3; Rom. 9: 5; 1 Cor. 8: 4, 6; Rev. 19: 6.

[4] Ps. 76: 10; Dn. 4: 25; Eph. 1: 11; Rev. 4: 11.

[5] Ps. 33: 6; Heb. 11: 3.

When man fell into sin, he was pursued by God's gracious initiative and intervention.[6] In Christ, the Mediator and Saviour appointed before the foundation of the world, he can again receive the light of revelation[7] and experience personal redemption. When restored to the knowledge and enjoyment of God, the redeemed man becomes aware that the saving work of Christ is all 'to the praise of his glorious grace'.[8] For, apart from His attributes of mercy, the divine Lord might well have acted very differently. He has been pleased, however, to be gracious and to make known His saving grace to sinners. In the same way, all are in His hands for the future. All are finally answerable to Him as Judge, and He will have the last word in settling men's eternal destiny.[9]

These truths are never seen in the Bible as in any way contrary to the truth (taught with equal plainness) that man is morally responsible before God. If God's sovereignty is made into a kind of fatalism, this is plainly unbiblical and is nearer to Islam than to New Testament Christianity.

The Bible

The divine inspiration and infallibility of Holy Scripture, as originally given, and its supreme authority in all matters of faith and conduct.

Christian belief about the Bible is the third item in the Basis. This order is deliberate. Unless we believe in the Triune God who reveals Himself to men, we shall find the teaching about the Bible baffling. In the nature of

---

[6] Mk. 10: 45; Tit. 3: 4-6; Heb. 1: 1, 2; 1 Pet. 1: 20.
[7] For more extended comments on revelation, see pp. 19ff.
[8] Eph. 1: 6; *cf.* Jn. 17: 1-4.
[9] 1 Pet. 4: 5.

the case, what one believes about the Bible will depend on what one believes about the God of the Bible.

a. 'Holy Scripture'

'Holy Scripture' in the Basis means the sixty-six books listed as canonical in the historic Protestant confessions.[1] The Apocryphal books are excluded, because they are not in the same category. There is no reason to believe that they are inspired in the same sense as canonical books and there are plenty of reasons for doubting it.

In treating these sixty-six books as the *canon* — that is, the rule or standard of teaching — the church obeys its Master; for both Testaments come to us backed by the personal authority of the Lord Jesus Christ.

The Old Testament was Jesus' Bible, which He quoted and obeyed throughout His ministry as instruction from His heavenly Father. Hereby He authenticated it for His followers as part of the rule for their own faith and life. That Jesus' Bible consisted of precisely the thirty-nine books which make up our Old Testament is really beyond doubt.[2]

The New Testament books are apostolic witness to Christ, guaranteed true and authoritative by the commission and promise of our Lord Himself.[3] Jesus

[1] See French Confession, Article III (1559); Belgic Confession, Article IV (1561); Article VI of the Thirty-Nine Articles (1563); Westminster Confession, chapter I: ii (1647).
[2] See 'The Canon of the Old Testament' (E. J. Young) and 'The Apocrypha' (G. D. Young) in C. F. H. Henry (ed.), *Revelation and the Bible* (1959); 'Canon of the Old Testament' (N. H. Ridderbos) in *The New Bible Dictionary* (1962).
[3] See Jn. 14: 26; 15: 26f.; 16: 13f.; 17: 20 and see J. W. Wenham, *Christ and the Bible* (1972).

charged the apostles in a quite unique way, and equipped them by the Spirit, to declare the truth about Him authoritatively in His name.[4] The early Christians saw that apostolic witness to Christ was no less authoritative when written than when spoken. Discussion in the early Christian centuries as to which books were canonical turned on the issue of apostolicity;[5] the books accepted were those shown to be written either by apostles or by men whose links with the apostles were such as to make it certain that the doctrine they taught was apostolic.

The canon is therefore closed, because the apostolic office of first-hand witness to the risen Christ is, in the nature of the case, at an end.[6] In the church today, the Holy Spirit works to give understanding of the Scriptures that now exist, not to add to their number. By this means the Holy Spirit makes Christ's presence real and applies His authority in day-to-day experience.

We do not need to add to the Bible because it is sufficient. Paul, in 2 Timothy 3: 13-17, argues not only that in a time of great variety of doctrine and practice we are to go back to the apostolic teaching and to the Old Testament ('what you have learned' and 'the sacred writings'). He also adds that these are given that 'the man of God may be complete, equipped for every good work'. We need living exposition and application of the Bible, but we do not need any fresh authoritative teaching. Indeed we *must* not add to the Bible, for any addition would, as experience shows,

---

[4] See Gal. 1: 11f.; 1 Cor. 2: especially vv. 12f.; 9: 16f.; 14: 37f. On the connection between apostolicity and authority, see J. N. Geldenhuys, *Supreme Authority* (1953).
[5] See 'Canon of the New Testament' (H. Ridderbos) in *Revelation and the Bible*; 'Canon of the New Testament' (J. N. Birdsall) in *The New Bible Dictionary*.
[6] See 'Apostle' (A. F. Walls) in *The New Bible Dictionary*.

only detract from and almost certainly conflict with what God has given. All the proposed additions have, at the very least, altered the balance of biblical teaching, and if they did not do so, would not need to be added.

It cannot be too strongly stressed that the only reliable first-hand testimony to the Person, teaching and work of Christ that is available to us is that of the Bible. This alone must give the Bible a unique place in our thought and life.

b. 'Divine inspiration'

Scripture, we see, has the character of witness — witness to God, to His nature, His work, His truth and His will, and in particular to the Person and work of Jesus Christ. This witness is not simply man's witness to God; it is also, and equally, God's own witness to Himself. The biblical books are not just human products. God is their true and ultimate author. Like Jesus Christ (though in a different manner) they are both fully human and fully divine. It is to this fact that the term 'inspiration' points, when applied to Scripture. It is quite distinct from the use of the word as applied to works of human genius or art. The Greek word *theopneustos*, translated 'given by inspiration of God' in 2 Timothy 3: 16 (AV), means 'breathed out by God':[7] it characterizes the Scriptures (in this case, those of the Old Testament) as products of the divine 'breath' which made the heavens (*cf.* Ps. 33: 6), and so as utterances of God in the same sense as were the prophetic oracles, introduced by 'thus says the Lord'. The New Testament authors constantly quote the Old Testament (not only the recorded statements of

[7] See B. B. Warfield, *The Inspiration and Authority of the Bible* (1948), chapters 3 and 6.

God, but also human statements as well) as being the word of God, or what God or the Holy Spirit says — in other words, as being of divine, and not merely human, origin, and as bearing a divine, and not merely human, message.[8]   Inspiration may therefore be defined as 'a supernatural, providential influence of God's Holy Spirit upon the human authors which caused them to write what He wished to be written'.[9]

Some modern theology has found difficulty with this idea, as with the idea of prophetic and apostolic inspiration in all its forms, mainly because of doubts as to whether God could conceivably communicate with men in words.   But if Jesus, the Galilean teacher, was God come in the flesh, then God's will to use language in addressing us is proved; for Jesus' words were words of God.   In fact, the Bible witnesses to verbal address by God to men right through from Genesis to Revelation.   To build theories of revelation and communion with God, or accounts of the Bible, on the assumption that God never communicates truth in words is therefore groundless.   God's revelation may be more than the bare meaning conveyed by the words. But it is not less.   Words are normally its basis and often its sole basis.   Love, for instance, is more than words about love, but without words we would know neither the fact nor the qualities of God's love.

Being divinely inspired, the Bible is not only a record of revelation in history, but is itself revelation in writing. It not only contains the word of God, it *is* the Word of God and that is true whether we grasp its truth or

[8] *Cf.* Mt. 19: 4f.; Mk. 7: 13; Jn. 10: 34f.; Acts 1: 16; 4: 25; 28: 25; Rom. 1: 2; 3: 2; 9: 6; *cf.* v. 17; 1 Cor. 10: 11; Heb. 1: 8; 3: 7; 8: 5, 8; 10: 15; 2 Pet. 1: 20f.; *etc.*   See 'Inspiration' (J. I. Packer) in *The New Bible Dictionary*.
[9] J. I. Packer, *'Fundamentalism' and the Word of God* (1958), p.77.

not. The depth and fullness of different passages vary as do the literary styles and methods of their various authors, but the fact of divine control and super-intendence over each writer remains constant. To speak of *control* in this connection is not to suggest that being inspired always meant for the author being psychologically passive. Ordinarily, indeed, the reverse was true, for God used each man's personality and active thoughts to the full. Nor does this use of human agents imply that from God's standpoint the resulting product was inadequate. God in His sovereignty prepared each writer by natural endowments, education and experience to make him capable, when the time came, of producing exactly what He had planned for the conveying of His truth. Having said this, however, we must agree that God's way of interacting with and controlling each writer's mind in its spontaneous movement is not explained in Scripture any more than is God's method of ordering and overruling all other free human acts. Peter simply says that the writers were 'impelled by the Holy Spirit'.[1]

The view of Scripture outlined above is sometimes called 'propositional revelation'. The phrase is from one standpoint less than happy, since most of Scripture consists of factual narration, poems, sermons, prayers and such like, rather than formal theological proposi-tions — though propositional statements can be found in considerable numbers, and the rest of Scripture can be shown to assume, illustrate and confirm them. However, the claim that God's revelation is proposi-tional was never meant to imply that all the books of Scripture have a uniform literary character. What the claim means is that whatever Scripture, in all its literary

[1] 2 Pet. 1: 21 (NEB).

variety, *tells us* is being told us by God Himself. Scripture, in other words, is 'the instruction of God'.

We accept biblical inspiration as a matter of faith in just the same way as we accept any other element in biblical teaching. The objective testimony to inspiration by a series of God-taught teachers — prophets, psalmists and apostles, for instance — comes home to us with assurance as divine truth through the inner witness of the Holy Spirit. This is equally true of the objective witness of the New Testament writers to the deity and saviourhood of the Lord Jesus Himself.

It is sometimes said that this view of biblical inspiration is inadmissible, being based on circular reasoning: the demonstration of it from the Scriptures assumes the inspiration of those Scriptures, and thus we presuppose what we have to prove. But this criticism is confused. The argument is a spiral and not a circle. It leads to increased confidence in Scripture as we progress. The questions 'what does Scripture teach about inspiration?' and 'is that teaching true?' are distinct, and we have so far tried only to answer the former, and not the latter. There is in fact a prior question, making three stages of the argument.

First, then, must we accept the New Testament as sound historical evidence for what Jesus and His disciples believed and taught? There are several good reasons for assuming this. Reconstructions of the documents to fit different philosophical and religious schemes are at the very best highly speculative and never more convincing than the originals. We really must treat the primary data with integrity and try honestly to see what they say. Then, since one of the major effects of Christianity has been to create a new respect for truth, it would be extremely strange if the New Testament writers deliberately lied or juggled with the data — partly in order to teach us a new respect for truth and reliability. The writers give every sign (and Luke, for instance, explicitly professes it[2]) of having gone to a lot of trouble to present a true picture and it is hard to see how they could have done otherwise, in view of the eternal significance of what they tell us. Finally we may be driven to respect the New Testament as authentic because through it we were brought to a knowledge of God in Christ. It has brought such light and life to us that we cannot regard it as merely an ordinary book. It is unique and it has mediated a new experience of God through what it states and teaches. We cannot allow that it is merely a collection of human ideas. It has transforming power and we can confidently accept its good faith.

Secondly, as we have shown, Jesus and His apostles constantly assumed and explicitly taught the inspiration and authority of both the apostolic writings and the Old Testament writings.[3] There is no real doubt about that if the documents were written in good faith.

Even if we are unwilling to rely on any particular verse or phrase it is quite clear that this doctrine of Scripture was an integral part of primitive Christianity. Some aspects of teaching might be dropped without totally changing the whole, but we cannot mistake the teaching of Christ and His apostles on this matter and we cannot delete it without wrecking the whole picture of truth. To disagree on this doctrine is to reject a corner-stone of New Testament Christianity. Most people would so far agree that this is in fact what Jesus and His apostles taught.

[2] Lk. 1: 1-4.
[3] *E.g.* 2 Tim. 3: 14-17

Finally, one has to ask whether it is safe to take the word of Jesus and His apostles on this matter. The real battle lies here.[4] If Jesus was wrong about this, He was fundamentally wrong. If He is accepted as an authority in matters of truth — if we are prepared to say that Jesus is our Lord — then He is to be believed and followed in this question as much as on all other fundamental truths, such as the doctrines of forgiveness, the love of God, eternal life and judgment. Also it is the same Holy Spirit who opens our eyes to see the truth of the deity and saviourhood of Christ who equally enables us to see and accept the truth of the divinity of Scripture and the other teachings of the Lord and His apostles. Some biblical truths are more *easily* acceptable than others in each particular age, but they all stand on the same footing.

This doctrine of the special inspiration of Scripture of course leads us back to study it and seek to understand and obey it with a new confidence which a mere acceptance of its *bona fides* could not supply. But we do not assume inspiration before we start. We progress from the good faith of the writers, through Jesus' explicit teaching, to the acceptance of inspiration because Jesus taught it.

c. 'Infallibility'

Infallibility, whether ascribed to persons or documents, is the quality of neither being deceived nor deceiving, and so of being entirely trustworthy. The application of the word to the Bible is at least as old as Wycliffe, who spoke of Holy Scripture as 'the infallible rule of truth' (*infallibilis . . . regula veritatis*). Among other

[4] See J. W. Wenham, *Christ and the Bible*.

doctrinal Confessions the Westminster Confession speaks of 'the infallible truth and divine authority thereof'; so the Basis, we may say, is in good company and has sound historical precedent when it makes its own use of the word.[5]

Infallibility — total trustworthiness — is entailed by the kind of inspiration that is clearly taught in the Bible. If God Himself is infallible, and is the ultimate author of Scripture, then Scripture will be infallible too. Infallibility is a personal and not a mechanical quality. If the word has in the minds of some people a coldly formal or machine-like quality, that is not what the Reformers (or the IVF Basis) intended when they used it. Language is spoken by *people* and God speaking is infallible in the same way as He is infallible Himself.

Not that every statement recorded in Scripture will therefore be true! The biblical narrative includes many false statements, *e.g.* those of the Pharisees and Jewish leaders against Jesus. The context, and the over-all viewpoint of the book from which they come, will ordinarily indicate the falsity of such statements. It is in each case the book itself and its affirmations that are inspired and infallible, not those who appear in the story unless the story itself specifically indicates this.

Some people suggest that this position is adopted in order to make interpretation easier. But belief in biblical infallibility will not in itself make a man a good interpreter of Scripture. It will help only if he is also careful, patient, humble and hard-working in his study of the text.

This exposes one of the problems. Many people want the Bible to be, like the Koran, a collection of

[5] Westminster Confession, I: v; J. I. Packer, *'Fundamentalism' and the Word of God*, pp. 94f.; and note 1 on p.95.

proof texts for every situation and problem. They feel that unless it can be said to deal with everything authoritatively it is not a worthy authority. But that for the most part is not how God has been pleased to deal with us. The revelation is above all in Christ. It is often given in propositions, sometimes in black and white rules and fixed points, but not always in any of these forms has God chosen to speak. Therefore we have to try humbly to understand and to apply what He has said, and we need to use our fallible minds in the process. We are not merely machines de-coding a computer programme into typed instructions. God *speaks* (talks) to His children. We are to respond as children to His infallible and authoritative voice as soon as we understand what He is saying. But like children we do not always get it right. That is our fault, not His. We do not always listen carefully enough or think over what we have heard before we act.

It is true that a capacity for spiritual discernment remains in the last analysis the decisive factor for understanding the Bible,[6] and that an uneducated seeker after God may often come straight to the meaning while an expert in linguistic or historical research may stumble over the obvious. It is also true, however, that it is the *meaning* of Scripture, strictly speaking, which is infallible, and to discover that meaning with exactness requires devout and scholarly labour. The meaning is in the words,[7] but we must dismiss as a dangerous superstition the idea that belief in the infallibility of biblical teaching makes the task of interpretation magically easy, or gives us a right to twist or allegorize texts and impose on them meanings suggested by pious fancy. We must recog-

[6] See, *e.g.*, 1 Cor. 2.
[7] See 1 Cor. 2: 13.

25

nize, rather, that belief in the infallibility of the text does not secure infallibility in the interpreter. Because the teaching of Scripture is in a totally different class from human ideas, he needs to watch most carefully against reading into the text his own ideas which cannot fairly be read out of it.

Equally the suggestion that belief in an infallible Bible makes one intellectually lazy is (or should be) the reverse of the truth. If it is infallible, then it is uniquely worth studying. As a scientist gets off the ground only when he has some reliable results to work with, so the Christian thinker's task really begins when he has reliable data to start from. The history of the church supplies ample proof that the greatest stimulus to fruitful thinking has frequently come just from this belief that the Bible is infallible and therefore must be understood and applied accurately, extensively and strenuously.

The fact of biblical inspiration and infallibility bears on our attitude to the historical narratives of Scripture. God revealed Himself in history, and the Bible is the interpretative record of the process. Any attempt to isolate the Bible's spiritual teaching from its historical context, endorsing the former as true but not the latter, is misguided. Doctrine and history, event and interpretation, are inextricably intertwined in Scripture. Our Lord made frequent references to Old Testament events, as well as to Old Testament teaching, and sometimes the point of His argument depended entirely on their historicity.[8] True as it may be that one could withhold assent from some historical statements in the Bible without wholly losing the faith, the fact remains that if we take seriously Jesus' dictum,

[8] See Mt. 12: 41; Lk. 11: 50f.; and J. W. Wenham, *Christ and the Bible.*

'scripture cannot be broken',[9] we shall not withhold assent from any of them. (This still leaves us with the necessity of understanding accurately what the Scriptures state.)

The supernatural character of many events recorded in the Bible raises the question of the relation of Scripture to science.[1] The Bible is not, of course, scientific in the sense of purporting to tell us the laws of natural phenomena. It tells us other things, for instance that all the universe is under God's sovereign control and all its phenomena, ordinary and extraordinary, recurring and unique, regular and miraculous, are alike expressions of His activity. Scripture and nature, being both products of the one true God, cannot conflict in reality, though their interpreters may sometimes do so through failure to read one or both aright. We should, however, note that whereas science is concerned with exhibiting the laws by which natural phenomena are related to each other, the concern of Scripture is on the whole with the relation of all the phenomena to God. Science in general asks *how*, Scripture in general explains *why*. Natural science and biblical theology are thus complementary, the latter interpreting in terms of God's activity and purpose the findings of the former.

When biblical writers touch the realms to which science nowadays lays claim, they speak reliably though they use the popular and pre-scientific language of their own time. What else could they have done? Of Old Testament cosmological language which pictures heaven as literally above the sky (the firmament) and Sheol (Hades, the place of the departed) as

[9] Jn. 10: 35.
[1] Many of these issues are discussed in B. Ramm, *The Christian View of Science and Scripture* (1955).

literally below ground, and of its physiological way of describing psychological experience — bones speaking, bowels yearning, kidneys instructing, *etc.* — it has been well written: 'It may be doubted whether these forms of speech were any more "scientific" in character and intent than modern references to the sun rising, or light-headedness, or walking on air, or one's heart sinking into one's boots, would be. It is much likelier that they were simply standard pieces of imagery, which the writers utilized, and sometimes heightened for poetic effect, without a thought of what they would imply for cosmology and physiology if taken literally. And language means no more than it is used to mean.'[2] Some interpreters seem to think that the biblical writers employed language in an entirely wooden and almost inhuman way. They try to make the writers teach things which do not seem to have been any part of what they were *meaning to say.* And that is what we always want to know: What does the passage intend to state? what does it mean? This rarely has a large scientific content though it may often include matters of fact and of history, and these are described reliably *in its own idiom* (*e.g.* population numbers are often rounded up or down to the nearest thousand).

d. 'As originally given'

The inclusion of words such as these in a doctrinal statement is sometimes seen as an evasive technique of locating inspiration where it is inaccessible to inspection, since the original manuscripts of the biblical books no longer exist. The real purpose of these words, however, is not to evade but to define. If inspiration

[2] J. I. Packer, *'Fundamentalism' and the Word of God,* p.97, note 2.

was a work of God in and upon the biblical authors, it applies essentially to the documents which they themselves wrote (or, in some cases, dictated and, presumably, then checked). Copyists and translators were not guaranteed the same kind of protection from error, and there is nothing infallible about the slips and inaccuracies which crept into their work of transmission. Though the Greek and Hebrew text is remarkably well preserved, scientific textual criticism is still needed to eliminate the occasional copyists' slips and get back to the wording of the inspired original. The labours of textual scholars have now made our level of certainty regarding the original text very high indeed.[3]

Nevertheless there remain a few obscure phrases where we cannot be sure of the meaning, either because we have lost some ancient idiom or because the original text is uncertain. No doctrine or practice should be based on a passage of doubtful meaning or a doubtful translation. Our confidence is in God's Word as originally given, and in the vast majority of passages its meaning is clear. But unless we make this distinction we could be at the mercy of faulty translators (*e.g.* those who put 'do penance' for 'repent').

A problem for believers in inspiration is sometimes thought to be raised by the freedom with which writers of the New Testament occasionally quote from the Old.[4] But if the inspired writer remains faithful to the thought of the passage he quotes, he is not to be blamed for employing a measure of paraphrase in his translation. All translators do the same, more or less. In fact, many of these quotations are of the 'pesher' type, combining quotation with interpretation — a

[3] See F. F. Bruce, *The Books and the Parchments* (1960).
[4] *E.g.* Eph. 4: 8; Heb. 10: 5-7.

type of quotation which was as common among the Jews as it is today in Christian sermons, and which appears equally legitimate in both cases.[5]

e. 'Supreme authority'

Authority — that is, the right to rule us — belongs to God, and God's authority is expressed in and through the inspired Scriptures.   Neither reason nor religious experience nor church tradition may be set above them; rather, Scripture must be allowed to judge and where necessary to correct all three.

To bow to the supreme authority of Holy Scripture is not bibliolatry, as is sometimes alleged. The Christian way is not worship of a book, but acceptance of the authority of the book as a basic part of our worship of God because this is God's Word. Psalm 119 is an eloquent commentary on this.

The relation of church tradition to the authority of Scripture needs closer definition. Jesus distinguished 'the word of God' (commands of Scripture) from the rabbinic 'traditions of men', ascribing authority to the former and denying it to the latter.[6] The tradition of the apostles — that is, their transmitted teaching — is, however, part of the Word of God and is authoritative for Christians at all times.[7] Church traditions of later ages should be seen, not as a second source of divine teaching to supplement Scripture (as the Church of Rome has for long supposed), but as, at best, a series of attempts (not always successful) to interpret and express biblical faith. The adequacy of these attempts is

[5] See F. F. Bruce, *Biblical Exegesis in the Qumran Texts* (1959);
E. E. Ellis, *Paul's Use of the Old Testament* (1957).
[6] Mk. 7: 6ff., 13.
[7] *Cf.* 2 Thes. 2: 15; 3: 6.

something which the Bible itself must be allowed in every case to judge.

To speak of the Bible *judging* is to imply that the Bible is essentially clear, self-interpreting, and able to speak for itself. On all that is essential this is indeed so, through the illumination given by the Holy Spirit who inspired it.

Knowing this, the Christian interpreter will seek to be teachable and receptive. He will set himself to follow out each writer's intended meaning, and to bring to bear upon modern life what he thus learns of God's will and ways. He will allow Scripture to expose and correct his own presuppositions, and progressively bring his thinking into line with its own. He will make it a matter of conscience to trust the biblical promises and to obey the biblical commands, and to bring his own problems to the Bible for resolution and guidance. He will labour, by God's grace, to cultivate in himself humility, openness of mind to new insight in the realm of biblical truth, responsiveness of heart, and a constant dependence upon the Spirit of God. Thus he will increasingly verify in his own experience the apostolic dictum: 'all Scripture is inspired by God and profitable for teaching, for reproof, for correction, and for training in righteousness, that the man of God may be complete, equipped for every good work.'[8]

f. *'In all matters of faith and conduct'*

It must be emphatically stated that faith and conduct belong together. If we abandon biblical truth we shall not be able to maintain Christian life for long. Equally, biblical teaching is meant to be practical. As 2

[8] 2 Tim. 3: 16, 17.

Timothy 3: 16, 17 reminds us, it is for both life and thought. It is 'for teaching, for reproof, for correction, and for training in righteousness, that the man of God may be complete'. If we allow our discussion of Christianity to stop at a theoretical level we are unbiblical. But as the pattern of most of the New Testament Epistles shows, the practical application and the worship and evangelism arise out of the doctrine. It is because God is as He is and man is in the state he is that 'I appeal to you *therefore,* by the mercies of God, to present your bodies as a living sacrifice, holy and acceptable to God.'[9]

This IVF Basis is, we believe, following biblical precedent in seeking to crystallize out first, and to express succinctly, the doctrinal foundation of Christianity on which all else is built. It does not attempt also a summary of the Christian life, partly because the New Testament seems to discourage such attempts as easily being distorted into legalism, while it has no hesitation about summaries of doctrine. This is not in any way to make conduct of secondary importance, as this clause is intended to show.

[9] Rom. 12: 1.

3 Man and his redemption

The second group of clauses in the Basis refers to the sin of man, his estrangement from God and his redemption. Reference is made below to those points at which a student may find most difficulty.

The fall of man

The universal sinfulness and guilt of human nature since the fall, rendering man subject to God's wrath and condemnation.

The Bible presents the fall of man as a historical event. The record in Genesis 3 describes (i) man as a creature of God and as responsible to Him, (ii) the giving of a clear Word of guidance to man concerning the conduct of his life and (iii) a deliberate act of disobedience to this divine Word, through which man lost the favour of God. The New Testament writers accept the fact of this act of rebellion and build upon it when presenting the Christian gospel.[1] There have been in modern times numerous alternative explanations and theories which, however, are without proof. The account in Genesis does not present a mere pictorial representation of some general 'tribal' or racial wrongdoing. It is also not in keeping with biblical teaching to regard the fall of man as an incident which marked an upward movement in moral consciousness. Theories which suggest that there was a gradual and inevitable advance in moral sense, and that there has been no catastrophic deterioration of man's moral nature as a result of the rebellion by our first parents are, also, contrary to the teaching of Scripture. They all fail to explain the observable tendency of all men to sin and the universal sense of blameworthiness.[2]

[1] Rom. 5: 12-21; 1 Cor. 15: 21, 22.
[2] Gn. 3; Rom. 1: 18 - 3: 20; 5: 12-21.

The Bible teaches that by an act of deliberate choice the first man sinned and became estranged from God. As a result he lost his enjoyment of fellowship with his Creator; and the whole of the human race, because it proceeds from him as its ancestor, has become morally disorganized.   Left to himself, man is incapable of reverting to the original condition of moral and spiritual harmony with God. He, however, is still a moral being, and possesses the capacity of estimating actions according to a standard of right and wrong. He still recognizes the obligation to goodness, even when he feels himself incapable of realizing it in practice. He is responsible to obey what he knows — either by nature through conscience or by special revelation through Scripture — to be the law of his Maker. The power of the gospel, brought home to the heart by the Holy Spirit, is alone capable of effecting man's deliverance from the blindness, dominion and pollution of his evil nature. Salvation means ultimately, and essentially, the removal by the work of Christ of the consequences of man's rebellion, the making of atonement, the opening of a way of reconciliation by the Mediator, the cleansing from the stain of sin and the readjustment of sinful man to the righteousness of God.

God's will, as regards man, is necessarily expressed in terms of law. This necessity arises from the fundamental relation between God and man. God's laws are not arbitrary, but exhibit His eternal righteousness in the form of His requirements from man. Those provisions which are inconvenient to man must not be separated off, and evaded, for the authority of the Lawgiver extends to each requirement.   Man sinned through listening to, and accepting, the suggestion of Satan that God's known requirements were unreasonable and unjust.

There are two important points to be borne in mind. It must first be emphasized that all men are by nature alienated from God[3] and prone to sin and, second, that whenever a man transgresses what he knows to be a plainly stated law of God, he is by that act a law-breaker. The resulting guiltiness is a permanent element in his relation to God.

The modern mind resists what both the Old and New Testaments categorically assert, namely, that God is 'angered' by sin. The Bible, indeed, constantly refers to what theologically is termed God's judicial displeasure against sin.[4] This is a fact with which we must come to terms. Wrath, in this sense, is as permanent an element in the divine nature as love. It is the reaction of holiness to unrighteousness. Because God is essentially righteous, fallen man — unrepentant and unredeemed — must be the object of His just condemnation.

Redemption

Redemption from the guilt, penalty and power of sin only *through the sacrificial death* (*as our Representative and Substitute*) *of Jesus Christ, the Incarnate Son of God.*

At the heart of the whole Christian message is the death of Christ. The crucial question which must be pressed upon all men everywhere is: 'Why did Jesus Christ, the Son of God, *die*?' Here lies the deepest mystery and the most profound truth of Christian theology. If Jesus were simply the greatest in the long line of prophets or of ethical philosophers, it is to some extent understandable that He should be martyred for His faith by a nation

[3] Rom. 1: 18 - 3: 20; 5: 12-21.
[4] Rom. 1: 18; 2: 5, 6; Col. 3: 6; *etc.*

which was notorious for its cruel treatment of its spiritual leaders and prophets. If He were but a mere man, it is conceivable that by courting martyrdom He might have designed to shame disordered humanity into doing the will of God by the 'moral influence' of His example. But the New Testament everywhere declares Him to have been more than a man and a prophet. The moment we admit Christ's claim to deity, such explanations are seen at once to be inadequate.

There are some modern theologians who dislike the biblical teaching concerning sacrifice and have reacted against what they call the 'sacrificial terms' of the New Testament. Others, even whilst they accept in the main the biblical concept, seem anxious to avoid the conclusion that Christ's death was either 'on our behalf' or 'in our stead'. Most modern 'theories' of the atonement fail to do justice to the impenetrable wonder of the fact that God the Son came into the world in order eventually 'to go to Jerusalem'[5] and of set purpose to give His life 'a ransom for many'.[6] The biblical record demands an explanation which will come to terms with: (i) the fact that a Person of the Sacred Trinity came into the world to put away sin; (ii) the nature and extent of human sin; and (iii) the absolute necessity and sufficiency of Christ's death to put away sin, to reconcile the sinner to God, and to restore him into His presence.

It is vital that we start by recognizing the identity of the central Person in the unique event enacted at Calvary. We shall therefore consider separately the main phrases of the sentence at the head of this section.

[5] Lk. 9: 51.
[6] Mk. 10: 45; 1 Tim. 2: 6; 1 Pet. 2: 24.

a. 'The Incarnate Son of God'

Jesus Christ was, and is, the eternal Son of God, who was conceived of the Holy Ghost and born of the Virgin Mary. He was, and is, true and perfect Man and perfect God. He combines two natures in the indissoluble unity of one Person.[7]

No part of revelation is of such importance as that which relates to the Person and work of Jesus Christ. Wrong views of His Person will mean wrong views about almost everything else. The New Testament makes it plain, not only that we have a revelation of God, but that Christ is the revelation. 'In him the whole fullness of deity dwells bodily.'[8] The manner of His coming to this world was supernatural, and His departure from it was supernatural. The miraculous conception and virgin birth of Jesus, His sinlessness and His miraculous resurrection and ascension are plainly recorded facts. Authentic witness is borne to them all in the New Testament. A study of the relevant passages makes this clear.[9]

b. 'Sacrificial death'

Several interpretations of the death of Christ have been put forward in an attempt to do justice to the variety of references which are found in the New Testament, such as that by His obedience to the will of God and His suffering even to death, He left us an example.[1] But for the purposes of the Doctrinal Basis, the most important aspects of the saving work of our Lord are that He died

[7] Mt. 1; Lk. 2; Jn. 20: 31; Rom. 8: 3; Eph. 1: 19-23; Phil. 2: 5-11; Col. 1: 15-19; Heb. 1; 2.
[8] Col. 2: 9.
[9] See, for example, Leon Morris, *The Lord from Heaven* (1958).
[1] Phil. 2: 5-8; 1 Pet. 2: 21.

as our *Representative* and that He died as our *Substitute.*

i. *Representative.* The representative nature of our Lord's Person and work is shown in such statements as: 'There is one God, and there is one mediator between God and men, the man Christ Jesus, who gave himself as a ransom for all.'[2] In a similar manner, the well-known passage in Romans 5 depends for its meaning upon the contrast between the disobedience, sin and death which came through Adam, and the obedience, grace, gift of righteousness and of life which came through Christ. The New Testament refers also to our Lord as 'the last Adam', 'the second man . . . from heaven'.[3] In this sense our Lord Jesus Christ may be spoken of as the first Representative Man in the new order of mankind, which has been inaugurated by His death and resurrection. He is the Head of 'the new creation'.[4]

ii. *Substitute.* No explanation of the cross of Christ which omits the idea of 'substitution' is adequate to do justice to the data presented to us in the books of the Bible. It seems plain from the Gospels that both our Lord and His disciples looked upon His death in the light of a transaction of which the Old Testament sacrifices were illustrations and types. 'The Son of man came. . . to give his life as a ransom for many.' 'This is my blood of the new covenant, which is poured out for many for the forgiveness of sins.'[5]

The fact that Christ was Son of God, as well as Son of man, of itself implies that there is a deep significance in His death. The language which the Bible uses in its explanations of the redeeming work of Christ invites us to search further. A careful collation of the New

[2] 1 Tim. 2: 5.   [3] 1 Cor. 15: 45, 47.
[4] Rom. 8: 29; Col. 1: 15.   [5] Mt. 20: 28; 26: 28.

Testament passages referring to Christ's death[6] (such as that, for example, presented by the late Dr James Denney in his book *The Death of Christ*) compels belief in an objective vicarious sacrifice whose character is adequately expressed only by a word such as 'substitution'. It is put by the apostle Peter in the following form — 'he himself bore our sins in his body on the tree',[7] and that He 'died for sins once for all, the righteous for the unrighteous, that he might bring us to God'.[8] In other words, the apostles taught that the divine judgment due to men for their sins was voluntarily endured in their place by the Son of God come in human form. We are convinced that the modern mind resists the principle of substitution, not because it is insufficiently stated in the Bible, which it is not, but because the deity of Christ is not sufficiently taken into account in relation to it. There is a mistaken notion that to talk in terms of substitution is 'immoral'; and so it would be if it were merely one man's life being substituted for another's. A human system of justice does not permit this. But it must be seen that 'God was in Christ reconciling the world to himself'.[9] Another reason for resistance to the idea is that man is unwilling to admit the radical nature of sin and his complete helplessness to save himself. Human pride rebels even at this point. It will not bow down and receive the gifts of God's mercy.

The doctrine of substitution truly stated emphasizes the fact that the Lord Jesus has exhausted the consequences of our sin in His own Person.[1] It is not a question of a *quantitative* equivalent, *i.e.* an equal

[6] Heb. 9; Mt. 20: 28; 2 Cor. 5: 21; Gal. 2: 20; 1 Pet. 3: 18; Rom. 5: 10; Phil. 2: 8; Heb. 2: 9-14; 1 Cor. 1: 23; Gal. 6: 12; Eph. 2: 16. *Cf.* also Lv. 16; Is. 53: 4-6.
[7] 1 Pet. 2: 24.   [8] 1 Pet. 3: 18.   [9] 2 Cor. 5: 19.
[1] Is. 53: 4-6; 1 Pet. 1: 19.

amount of punishment for the total quantity of human sins. The Bible itself repeatedly focuses attention on the divine *quality* of the sinless Substitute, of His meeting the basic requirements of God's moral government of the world and of His dealing with the root principle of sin.

A study of the sacrificial words which are used in the Greek New Testament, compared with those in the (Greek) Septuagint version[2] of the Old Testament, and a further comparison with their equivalents used in the Hebrew Old Testament, leave little room for doubt that the New Testament writers interpreted the death of Christ in terms of the Old Testament teaching. This is illustrated, for example, by the terms denoting expiatory 'sacrifice' (θυσία, see Eph. 5: 2; Heb. 10: 12); 'offering' (προσφορά, see Heb. 10: 10, 14); 'propitiation' (ἱλασμός, see Rom. 3: 25; 1 Jn. 2: 2); 'ransom' (λύτρον, see Mt. 20: 28; 1 Tim. 2: 6); 'redemption' (ἀπολύτρωσις, see Eph. 1: 7; Col. 1: 14); and 'reconciliation' (καταλλαγή, see Rom. 5: 10; 2 Cor. 5: 18-20; Eph. 2: 16-18). In addition, the apostles use very forceful expressions when describing Christ's work, such as 'made . . . sin for us' (2 Cor. 5: 21), 'become a curse for us' (Gal. 3: 13); and 'Christ . . . suffered . . ., the righteous for the unrighteous' (1 Pet. 3: 18).

c. 'Only'

The statement in this clause of the Basis, which affirms that redemption is secured *only* through the sacrificial

[2] The Septuagint was so named from the 'Seventy' Alexandrian scholars who are traditionally said to have completed a translation of the Hebrew Old Testament into Greek by the years 150-100 BC. It was the Greek Version in use at the time when the apostles were writing.

death of our Lord Jesus Christ, must be understood to mean that all human merit is entirely excluded from the grounds on which God forgives the sinner. The 'grace of renewal' (i.e. sanctification) also comes to us through the propitiation made on our behalf by Jesus Christ our Lord. The holiness wrought in us by the Spirit of God is not itself a ground of acceptance with God. We cannot become holy unless we have first received 'the righteousness of God in Christ'.

The outstanding truth to be grasped is (to borrow the words of James Denney) that the death of Christ is 'the centre of gravity in the New Testament'. He adds, 'Not Bethlehem, but Calvary, is the focus of revelation.' It is noteworthy that it is His death, not His life or teaching, which our Lord would have us perpetually to commemorate in His own ordinance of the Lord's Supper. It is necessary for Christians to be wisely and humbly uncompromising concerning this matter. For, as Denney goes on to say, 'If God has really done something in Christ on which the salvation of the world depends, and if He has made it known, then it is a Christian duty to be intolerant of everything which ignores, denies, or explains it away. The man who perverts it is the worst enemy of God and men.'

Resurrection

The resurrection of Jesus Christ from the dead.

The closing sections of each of the Gospels plainly teach that the crucified body of our Lord was raised from the tomb.[3] This claim, together with the facts concerning

[3] See J. N. D. Anderson, *The Evidence for the Resurrection* (1950), F. Morison, *Who Moved the Stone?* (1930), and Michael Green, *Man Alive!* (1967).

the death of Christ, became the central part of the witness of the apostles as shown in their addresses in the book of Acts. The event is described throughout the New Testament with a note of triumph as the completion and authentication of the value of His sacrifice.

The resurrection is an integral part of God's saving work. Easter morning is the complement of Good Friday and it symbolizes the victory of Christ. Christians are saved by His death and resurrection; they are united to Him in them both. The raising of Christ from the dead set the divine seal upon the sacrifice of Calvary, and vindicated Jesus' claim to be the Son of God.

Students, in discussing this subject, would be well advised to observe the reticence in matters of detail which Holy Scripture maintains when describing the form of our Lord's resurrection body. They should note, in particular, the way in which it is described in 1 Corinthians 15: 35 and the following verses. The evidence points to the fact that there was a resurrection of the physical body and there was not simply a survival of the disembodied spirit. The body which was buried was also raised, though it was in a transfigured form. There was both continuity and dissimilarity. The resurrection body was adapted to new spiritual conditions, but it was a result of the transformation of the natural body which had lain in the grave. If the evidence of the New Testament is closely followed,[4] the fact of the resurrection and the objective reality of the resurrection body will not be separated.

The resurrection not only demonstrated that God had accepted our Lord's sacrifice, it not only completed His victory over sin and death, but it is associated with a

[4] This will be found in the Gospels and in the Acts of the Apostles. See also Phil. 3: 20, 21; 1 Cor. 15: 43-49.

turning-point in the history of 'God's people'. Christ ascended into heaven and there acts on behalf of His people as their 'Priest' and 'Advocate' before God. Not only so, but as a result of His resurrection, He poured forth His Holy Spirit upon the church to be 'the Lord the Life-giver', 'the Comforter' and the Guide of His disciples in their pilgrimage through this world. They are invited to benefit from and to enter into 'the power of his resurrection'. This fact has great practical importance.[5]

When our Lord died the veil of the temple, which separated the worshipper from the inner sanctuary, was miraculously rent. This was to show that the way into the holiest was now open to those who are in Christ. The empty tomb revealed that death had no further dominion over Him. He could say to the dying thief, 'Today you will be with me in Paradise.' His resurrection and ascension completed His victory over death and has opened the way into God's presence for His people.[6]

[5] 1 Cor. 15: 12-22.
[6] Eph. 4: 8-13; Heb. 2: 14-18; 4: 14-16; 10: 19-25.

4 The Christian life and its consummation

The final clauses of the Basis deal with the Christian life, both in the individual and corporately in the church, and with its consummation. In these last sections it is the third Person of the Trinity whose activities take precedence.

Repentance and faith

The necessity of the work of the Holy Spirit to make the death of Christ effective to the individual sinner, granting him repentance toward God and faith in Jesus Christ.

The Christian is described in the New Testament as one who is 'born again' and has become a 'new creature'. This is contrasted with his previous condition in which he was 'dead in trespasses and sins'. This great change is an operation of the Holy Spirit.[1] It has been described as 'a radical and complete transformation wrought in the soul[2] by God the Holy Spirit,[3] by virtue of which we become "new men",[4] no longer conformed to this world,[5] but in holiness and knowledge of the truth created in the image of God'.[6] This great change is made real in experience as a result of what is known as the effectual call of God.[7] The call is normally mediated through the Holy Scriptures (read, preached or remembered), whereupon the Holy Spirit leads to awareness of sin, 'repentance unto life' and 'saving faith' in our Lord Jesus Christ. In such phrases the Bible describes the process by which a man becomes a Christian.[8]

[1] Jn. 16: 8-15; Acts 16: 14; 1 Cor. 2: 10-12; Eph. 2: 1-10.
[2] Rom. 12: 2; Eph. 4: 23.   [3] Tit. 3: 5.
[4] Eph. 4: 24; Col. 3: 10.   [5] Rom. 12: 2; Eph. 4: 22, 23.
[6] Quotation from B. B. Warfield.
[7] Acts. 2: 39; Rom. 8: 30.
[8] Ezk. 36: 26, 27; Jn. 3: 1-21; 2 Cor. 5: 17. For study, Rom. 8; Eph. 1.

The description of Lydia's conversion given in the Acts of the Apostles[9] illustrates how the Spirit of Christ works in the human heart: 'One who heard us was a woman named Lydia, . . . a seller of purple goods, . . . The Lord opened her heart to give heed to what was said by Paul.' If the reader observes the tenses in the Greek text, the description of the process becomes clearer. She 'was hearing' us (imperfect), whose heart the Lord 'opened' (aorist, *i.e.* a definite act of God), 'to give heed' (infinitive, *i.e.* a resulting purposeful act on her part). Whoever in this way receives Christ is 'born of God' and is God's child.[1] He has been 'born again',[2] because in Christ he has been translated into a new order of life. The important point which the New Testament emphasizes is that a man consciously becomes a Christian by receiving Jesus Christ as Saviour and Lord.[3]

Sanctification

The indwelling and work of the Holy Spirit in the believer.

The Spirit's presence in the heart and life of the individual is the God-given seal of his membership in the family of God.[4] It cannot be too strongly emphasized today, in view of the confusion which has been introduced by modern phraseology, that everyone who is really a Christian is indwelt by the Holy Spirit. The purpose of His indwelling is to renew in the believer what was lost by man at the fall, that is, the knowledge of God, righteousness and true holiness.[5] He is the Guide who is continually concerned to bring the

[9] Acts 16: 14.   [1] 1 Jn. 5: 1.   [2] Jn. 3: 3 (AV).
[3] Jn. 1: 12.   [4] Rom. 8: 9, 14-16.
[5] Eph. 4: 24; Col. 3: 10; Jn. 14: 16, 17, 26; Tit. 3: 5.

children of God into greater conformity of character with that of their heavenly Father.[6] The Holy Spirit is primarily concerned with ensuring our co-operation in the process of sanctification, *i.e.* a renewing in us of 'the image of God', which entails making us 'to be conformed to the image of his Son'.[7]

The distinction between the justification of the individual, who receives Christ, and his sanctification may be made clearer by the following summary by W. Griffith Thomas: 'The two are inseparable in fact, but they are distinguishable in thought. Justification concerns our standing; sanctification our state. The former affects our position (before God); the latter our condition. The first deals with relationship (to God); the second with fellowship (with God). Even though they are best wed together we must never confuse them. The one is the foundation of peace, "Christ for us"; the other is the foundation of purity, "Christ in us". The one deals with acceptance (with God); the other with attainment. Sanctification admits of degrees: we may be more or less sanctified; justification has no degrees, but is complete, perfect and eternal. "Justified from all things." Our Lord indicated this distinction,[8] when He said, "He that is bathed (justification) needeth not, save to wash his feet (sanctification)".'

But, as already stated, the Holy Spirit also fulfils a number of other functions, and all scriptural references to them deserve the most careful and prayerful consideration. For example, the Holy Spirit dwells in individual Christians making them 'partakers of the divine nature'.[9] This divine nature expresses itself in a growing likeness to the Lord Jesus Christ, 'the fruit

[6] Jn. 16: 7-15; 1 Jn. 2: 20, 27-29.
[7] Rom. 8: 29. [8] Jn. 13: 10. [9] 2 Pet. 1: 4.

of the Spirit'.[1] The Holy Spirit thus perfects Christian character. He also acts as the Interpreter of Scripture,[2] equips for Christian service,[3] and undertakes intercession for the Christian, whose own prayers are often so ill-informed.[4]

The third Person of the Trinity occupies a far more vital place in God's provision for His people than the majority of Christians appear to realize. Any adequate consideration would need to comprise a careful study[5] of the relationship of the Holy Spirit with (i) the Godhead, (ii) the church, (iii) the individual Christian, and (iv) the Scriptures.

In this connection we may make a brief reference to His work in the church. The Bible teaches us that the Holy Spirit dwells both in the local church[6] and in the universal church.[7] The one Spirit animates the whole church[8] and is the source of fellowship which unites Christians in the 'one body' of Christ. Further reference will be made below to the importance of an individual Christian's finding his spiritual completion in this fellowship of believers.[9]

There is often much misgiving in the young Christian's mind because his daily experience does not conform to what he thinks it ought to be in view of the Bible's promises. He finds he is not free from sinful thoughts, and may often meet temporary defeat in his war with evil. It is well to be reminded of the deep-seated effects of sin in man. Warnings concerning this are found in the Protestant Confessions of Faith; for example, 'This infection of nature doth remain, yea in them that are regenerated; whereby the lust of the flesh . . . is not

[1] Gal. 5: 22, 23.   [2] Jn. 16: 13.   [3] Acts 1: 8.   [4] Rom. 8: 26.
[5] 1 Cor. 3: 16 (cf. Rom. 12: 2); 2 Cor. 5: 17; 2 Pet. 1: 4;
Gal. 5: 16, 25; Rom. 15: 13; Acts 1: 8.
[6] 1 Cor. 3: 16.   [7] Eph. 2: 20-22.   [8] Eph. 4: 3, 4.   [9] See p. 49.

subject to the Law of God'.[1] Also, 'This sanctification is throughout in the whole man, yet imperfect in this life; there abideth still some remnants of corruption in every part: whence ariseth a continual and irreconcilable war; the flesh lusting against the Spirit, and the Spirit against the flesh. In which war, although the remaining corruption for a time may much prevail, yet, through the continual supply of strength from the sanctifying Spirit of Christ, the regenerate part doth overcome: and so the saints grow in grace, perfecting holiness in the fear of God'.[2]

---

[1] Article IX of the Church of England.
[2] Chapter XIII (Sections ii and iii) of the Westminster Confession.

5 The Church and Christ's second coming

The one holy universal Church, which is the Body of Christ, and to which all true believers belong.[1]

All who come to Christ in personal saving faith and acknowledge Him as Lord are made, by their new relationship with Him, members of the one, sanctified, world-wide company of His redeemed people.[2] For the Spirit of God, who gives them new life in Christ, in Him unites them with all who are similarly baptized by the one Spirit.[3] This community constitutes a body of which Christ is the Head.[4] They form a building or temple which is indwelt by God's Spirit.[5] They constitute a priesthood which is to offer the sacrifice of worship.[6] This 'people of God' has the duty to spread the wonderful knowledge of God's saving work.[7] In this community they are inter-dependent, or 'members one of another'.[8] They are intended to enjoy the fullness of their new life in Christ in active fellowship together; and thus to preserve, and openly to express, a unity which is God-given and already theirs in Christ.[9] Such fellowship is clearly meant to be realized, wherever possible, by every Christian by active membership in a local congregation.[1]

The Christian Unions affiliated to the Inter-Varsity Fellowship are not to be regarded as such local congregations or 'churches'. They have a limited purpose in a limited sphere and for a limited period in the experience of their members. They provide opportunities for fellowship and Bible study for Christian students who are temporarily thrown together during one important period of their lives. They are also centres of evangelistic witness with the same limitations. At

[1] For study, the Epistle to the Ephesians.
[2] Jn. 10:16; 1 Cor. 1: 2. [3] 1 Cor. 12: 13. [4] Eph. 1: 22, 23.
[5] Eph. 2: 20-22. [6] 1 Pet. 2: 5. [7] 1 Pet. 2: 9. [8] Rom. 12: 5.
[9] Eph. 4: 3, 13-16. [1] Heb. 10: 24, 25.

the same time, it is important that their members should not neglect regular participation in the worship and fellowship of a proper local expression of the Body of Christ. They ought normally to be baptized members, and to partake regularly of the Lord's Supper, in such a congregation.

This means that the Inter-Varsity Fellowship would wish earnestly to disclaim any notion that it is, or desires to become, a church or sect. Its functions are purely those of an auxiliary to the mainstream of church life. It is the duty and privilege of its members to encourage one another to work in true communion with any Christian congregation which is scriptural in preaching and practice, and whose members acknowledge the one Lord and confess the one faith.

A valuable feature of the work of the IVF from the beginning has been the fact that the Doctrinal Basis has been signed in all sincerity by individual members of many different denominations, and that denominational differences have not been allowed to weaken the united witness. It is most important that this state of affairs should continue. All officers and members are, therefore, urged to discourage any attempts within the Unions to proselytize, and to refrain from criticism or disparagement of the denominational views of other members. United opposition to fundamental error will be all the stronger if they are free to differ about secondary matters. At the same time, any member of a Christian Union who has no definite affiliation, for example, through being recently converted, should be encouraged to join a congregation of the Christian church. As a rule this will be that community under whose influence he has been brought up or through which he first effectually heard the call of God.

There are today movements towards increasing co-operation not only between local congregations, but between whole Christian denominations (which are often and wrongly called 'churches').   All must welcome effective co-operation among true Christians and pray for such unity, in loyalty to the truth, as will not sacrifice essential principle.   Whilst emphasizing the privilege and duty of fellowship with other Christians, in accordance with Acts 2: 42, it is necessary also to observe that no encouragement is given in the New Testament to those who would exalt fellowship at the expense of sound doctrine.

Christ's second coming

The expectation of the personal return of the Lord Jesus Christ.

The Scriptures clearly reveal that our Lord Jesus will return to the world in a manner similar to that in which He ascended from it.   While the details of this future event are subject to different interpretations concerning its form and the order of events, the promise of a future personal return is assured by Scripture. It is as indubitable as the fact of the first coming, and is the subject of a considerable number of references in both the Old and New Testaments.[2] As Dr W. Griffith Thomas has pointed out, in contrast with the paucity of reference to the Sacraments, 'The Lord's coming is referred to in one verse out of every thirteen in the New Testament, and in the Epistles alone in one verse out of ten.   This proportion is surely of importance, for if frequency of mention is any criterion there is scarcely any other truth of equal interest and value.'[3]

[2] Mt. 24; 25; Mk. 14: 62; Jn. 14: 3; Acts 1: 11; 1 Thes. 4: 13-18; 2 Thes. 1: 7-10; Mk. 13: 32; Lk. 17: 23, 24.
[3] W. H. Griffith Thomas, *The Principles of Theology* (1930), p.87 (footnote).

Throughout the ages there have been diverse interpretations of the prophecies concerning the second coming and hence a further comment is necessary. It must be emphasized that our Lord's 'coming' for a Christian at death does not begin to exhaust the meaning of the New Testament's reference to the second Advent. It is of cosmic importance. Scripture is also definite concerning the suddenness of this event. It will be 'as the lightning' flashing across the sky.[4] It is not possible to know the date, for this has not been revealed.[5] Our Lord's parables and Paul's exhortations emphasize the need for anticipation, watchfulness, industrious application to present duty and an increased purity of life in the light of this coming event.[6] It will be 'with power and great glory';[7] after it there will be no further opportunity of receiving the blessings of the gospel,[8] and all must appear before the judgment seat of God.[9] The expectation gives hope to the Christian and should spur him to further zeal in the spread of the gospel.

The second coming is the goal towards which all church history moves. Christians are instructed to await eagerly the arrival of their Lord, and to lead lives which are in conformity with their expectation.

[4] Mt. 24: 27.   [5] Mt. 24: 36.
[6] Mt. 24: 42 - 25: 46; Tit. 2: 11-15; Heb. 10: 23-25.
[7] Mt. 16: 27; 24: 30; Lk. 21: 27.
[8] Mt. 25: 10-12.   [9] Rom. 14: 10; 2 Cor. 5: 10.

6 The demands of the truth

a. *Witnessing to truth*

In the things of God, as in ordinary human affairs, many Christians are apt to take too much for granted. It is all too easy to believe in a general way that truth will prevail, and to do nothing to seek to ensure that it does. We must remind ourselves of the long periods of history when light seemed almost to have been extinguished by the powers of darkness. It was rekindled and the People of God could move forward again into a new day only through the fidelity and self-sacrifice of men who cared sufficiently to suffer so that truth might not perish from the earth. The Christian church has been rich in such men and women — saints, reformers and martyrs. It is through their vigilance and devotion that we can in our turn 'hold the faith' today. But each of us must see that we *do* hold it.

The effective method by which the gospel has come down to us is described in 2 Timothy 2: 1, 2: 'You then, my son, be strong in the grace that is in Christ Jesus, and what you have heard from me before many witnesses entrust to faithful men who will be able to teach others also.' In our generation such 'faithful men' are still needed, who will 'be able to teach others also'.[1] One of Paul's favourite metaphors to describe this responsibility to hand on the essentials of the tradition is that of keeping the 'deposit' (ἡ παραθήκη). The reference in 1 Timothy 6: 20 might accurately be translated 'O Timothy, guard the deposit'. When Paul wrote these words the greater part of the 'deposit' had been communicated orally. We have it now in written form so that we may be in no doubt concerning its reliability and may avoid the confusion arising from subsequent false traditions. There is today greater need than

[1] See also 1 Tim. 1: 18; 6: 13, 20.

ever to hold fast to the treasure of the saving truths of the gospel.

b. *Obeying the truth*

The Christian's attitude and actions must always be in keeping with his knowledge of the truth. The need for this was put very pointedly to the Pilgrim Fathers by their minister, John Robinson, on their taking leave in 1620:

'Brethren, we are now quickly to part from one another, and whether I may ever live to see your faces on earth any more the God of heaven only knows; but whether the Lord has appointed that or not, I charge you before God and His blessed angels, that you follow me no further than you have seen me follow the Lord Jesus Christ. If God reveal anything to you by any other instrument of His, be as ready to receive it as ever you were to receive any truth by my ministry; for I am verily persuaded the Lord has more truth yet to break forth out of His holy Word. For my part, I cannot sufficiently bewail the condition of the Reformed Churches, who are come to a period[2] in religion, and will go at present no further than the instrument of their reformation. The Lutherans cannot be drawn to go beyond what Luther saw; whatever part of His will our God has revealed to Calvin they will die rather than embrace it; and the Calvinists, you see, stick fast where they were left by that great man of God who yet saw not all things. This is a misery much to be lamented, for though they were burning and shining lights in their times yet they penetrated not unto the whole counsel of God, but were they now living would

[2] *i.e.* 'to a full stop'.

be as willing to embrace further light as that which they first received. I beseech you remember, it is an article of your Church covenant that you be ready to receive whatever truth shall be made known to you from the written Word of God.'

The apostle Paul, when taking final leave of the elders of the church at Ephesus, added to his call for faithfulness in matters of doctrine, a further appeal that their lives should match their theory.[3] 'For I did not shrink from declaring to you the whole counsel of God. Take heed to yourselves and to all the flock, in which the Holy Spirit has made you overseers, to care for the church of God which he obtained with the blood of his own Son. I know that after my departure fierce wolves will come in among you, not sparing the flock; and from among your own selves will arise men speaking perverse things, to draw away the disciples after them. Therefore be alert, remembering that for three years I did not cease night or day to admonish every one with tears. And now I commend you to God and to the word of his grace, which is able to build you up and to give you the inheritance among all those who are sanctified. I coveted no one's silver or gold or apparel. You yourselves know that these hands ministered to my necessities, and to those who were with me. In all things I have shown you that by so toiling one must help the weak, remembering the words of the Lord Jesus, how he said, "It is more blessed to give than to receive".'

[3] Acts 20: 27-35.

Appendix A

The Bible and the Protestant Confessions of Faith

The reader will find much more inspiration than he may anticipate by consulting the Confessions of Faith adopted by the Protestant churches at the time of the Reformation, and subsequently. They are masterpieces of short statement on the essentials of Christian doctrine, as anyone will discover, for example, who tries to re-write one of the Articles. It is worth noting how some of these Confessions deal with the nature and authority of Scripture, and the place that it should have in the life of the church and the Christian. The Thirty-nine Articles of the Church of England (which will be found printed at the end of the Book of Common Prayer) refer to the Bible in the following terms:

'Holy Scripture containeth all things necessary to salvation: so that whatsoever is not read therein, nor may be proved thereby, is not to be required of any man, that it should be believed as an article of Faith, or be thought requisite or necessary to salvation . . .' (Article VI).

and

' . . . And yet it is not lawful for the Church to ordain any thing that is contrary to God's Word written, neither may it so expound one place of Scripture, that it be repugnant to another. Wherefore, although the Church be a witness and a keeper of Holy Writ, yet, as it ought not to decree any thing against the same, so besides the same ought it not to enforce any thing to be believed for necessity of Salvation' (Article XX).

There are appeals to, and elucidations of the authority of, Scripture in Articles VII, VIII, XVII, XVIII, XIX, XXI, XXII, XXIV, XXV, XXVIII, XXXIV, XXXVII, XXXIX.

Later, by order of Parliament, and after working for three years, the leading theologians of the Church of England and of the Church of Scotland issued in 1647 the 'Westminster Confession' as a joint declaration of faith in which the Churches in Great Britain could unite. Chapter I of this Confession offers what is, perhaps, the best general statement on the nature and authority of Holy Scripture which is available to the English-speaking Churches. The following sections of Chapter I of this document are the most relevant to the purpose of this present booklet:

'Although the light of nature, and the works of creation and providence, do so far manifest the goodness, wisdom, and power of God, as to leave men inexcusable; yet they are not sufficient to give that knowledge of God, and of His will, which is necessary unto salvation; therefore it pleased the Lord, at sundry times, and in divers manners, to reveal Himself, and to declare that His will unto His church; and afterwards, for the better preserving and propagating of the truth . . . to commit the same wholly unto writing; which maketh the Holy Scripture to be most necessary . . . All things in Scripture are not alike plain in themselves, nor alike clear unto all; yet those things which are necessary to be known, believed, and observed, for salvation, are so clearly propounded and opened in some place of Scripture or other, that not only the learned, but the unlearned, in a due use of the ordinary means, may attain unto a sufficient understanding of them . . .

'The infallible rule of interpretation of Scripture is the Scripture itself; and therefore, when there is a question about the true and full sense of any Scripture (which is not manifold, but one), it must be searched and known by other places that speak more clearly.

'The supreme Judge, by which all controversies of religion are to be determined, and all decrees of councils, opinions of ancient writers, doctrines of men, and private spirits, are to be examined, and in whose sentence we are to rest, can be no other but the Holy Spirit speaking in the Scripture.'

The Savoy 'Declaration of the Faith and Order in the Congregational Churches in England' (1658), in adopting Chapter I of the Westminster Confession, makes a significant change in the last paragraph. It reads: 'The supreme Judge . . . in whose sentence we are to rest, can be no other, but the Holy Scripture delivered by the Spirit; into which Scripture so delivered, our Faith is finally resolved.' It will be seen at once that this is an uncompromising appeal to the authority of the letter of Scripture. The Bible is firmly placed in the position of being an objective standard, not to be modified by subjective or extraneous considerations.

In the Declaration of Faith, Church Order and Discipline of the Congregational or Independent Dissenters adopted at the Annual Meeting of the Congregational Union, 1833, the position is virtually unchanged. Clause I reads: 'The Scriptures of the Old Testament as received by the Jews, and the books of the New Testament, as received by the Primitive Christians from the Evangelists and Apostles, Congregational Churches believe to be divinely inspired and of supreme authority. These writings, in the languages in which they were originally composed, are to be consulted, by the aids of sound criticism, as a final appeal to all controversies; but the common version they consider to be adequate to the ordinary purposes of Christian instruction and edification.'

The Methodist Churches have continued officially to hold the Thirty-nine Articles as regulative. When John Wesley drew up the Twenty-five Articles of Religion for the American Methodists he followed closely the Articles in all such matters as reference to the Scriptures and main doctrines. When the Scheme of Union was drawn up to unite the three Methodist bodies in 1931, the position concerning ultimate doctrinal authority was worded as follows:

'The Doctrines of the Evangelical Faith, which Methodism has held from the beginning, and still holds, are based upon the Divine Revelation recorded in the Holy Scriptures. The Methodist Church acknowledges this revelation as the supreme rule of faith and practice. These Evangelical Doctrines to which the preachers of the Methodist Church, Ministerial and Lay, are pledged are contained in Wesley's Notes on the New Testament and the first four volumes of Sermons.'

Due mainly to their church polity, no *one* Confession of Faith has united all Baptist congregations, although these several Confessions have been in substantial agreement with Chapter I of the Westminster Confession. Thus the Confession of Particular Baptists in 1677 (Revised 1689) wholly follows Westminster in the doctrine of Scripture. The Confession of the General Baptists (1834) is in the form of a series of short statements, of which Clause I reads:

'The Holy Scriptures are the Old and New Testaments: they were written by holy men, inspired by the Holy Spirit, and contain God's revealed will to man. They are a sufficient and infallible guide in religious faith and practice.'

At the outset of the movement for church union in the late nineteenth century, the Anglican Bishops made an offer of church reunion, which has become known as 'The Lambeth Quadrilateral', because of its four tersely worded sentences. The first, on Holy Scripture, reads: 'The Holy Scriptures of the Old and New Testaments as containing all things necessary to salvation and as being the rule and ultimate standard of faith.'

There can be no doubt from the evidence of church

history that it is the fundamental principle of the life of the Protestant churches that the Word of God shall be revered and obeyed as the ultimate source and authority in Christian doctrine, practice and church government. The IVF seeks to uphold this basic confessional tenet of historic Protestantism.

Bibliography

The following bibliography is included in order to encourage all who use this booklet to read more deeply in Christian Doctrine. It is not intended to be complete, or a list for theological students, but has in mind the needs of younger Christians, who have little present acquaintance with the subject. The lists, therefore, contain the cheaper and more elementary type of book — except that in certain cases, *e.g.* the section on Systematic Doctrine, it is scarcely possible to adhere to this limitation.

The bibliography below is almost entirely confined to the books which were available through the book-shops at the time of compilation.

I. INTRODUCTORY

Hammond, T.C. *In Understanding Be Men* (IVP).
Lloyd-Jones, D.M. *Authority* (IVP).
Marshall, I.H. *Christian Beliefs* (IVP).
Moule, Handley C.G. *Outlines of Christian Doctrine* (Hodder and Stoughton. Secondhand only).
Stott, J.R.W. *Basic Christianity* (IVP).
Whyte, Alexander. *A Commentary on the Shorter Catechism* (T. & T. Clark).

II. SYSTEMATIC THEOLOGY

Baptist
Strong, A.H. *Systematic Theology* (Pickering and Inglis).

Brethren
Tatford, F.A. (Editor). *The Faith: A Symposium of Bible Doctrine* (Pickering and Inglis).

Church of England
Litton, E.A. *An Introduction to Dogmatic Theology*

(James Clarke).

Thomas, W.H. Griffith. *The Principles of Theology* (Church Book Room Press).

Methodist

Pope, W.B. *A Compendium of Christian Theology* (Wesleyan Methodist Book Room. 3 Vols. Second-hand only).

Presbyterian

Berkhof, L. *Systematic Theology* (Banner of Truth).

Calvin, J. *Institutes of the Christian Relgion* (James Clarke. 2 vols).

Hodge, C.H. *Systematic Theology* (James Clarke. 3 vols).

III. HOLY SCRIPTURE

Bruce, F.F. *The Books and the Parchments* (Pickering and Inglis).

Bruce, F.F. *The New Testament Documents* (IVP).

Douglas, J.D. *et al.* (Editors). *The New Bible Dictionary* (IVP).

Guthrie, D., Motyer, J.A., Stibbs, A.M. and Wiseman, D.J. (Editors). *The New Bible Commentary Revised* (IVP).

Henry, Carl C.H. (Editor). *Revelation and the Bible* (Tyndale Press).

Horn, R.M. *The Book that Speaks for Itself* (IVP).

Packer, J.I. *'Fundamentalism' and the Word of God* (IVP).

Packer, J.I. *God has Spoken* (Hodder and Stoughton).

Warfield, B.B. *The Inspiration and Authority of the Bible* (Marshall, Morgan and Scott).

Wenham, J.W. *Christ and the Bible* (Tyndale Press).

IV.   THE PERSON AND WORK OF CHRIST

Denney, James. *The Death of Christ* (Tyndale Press).
Morris, Leon. *The Apostolic Preaching of the Cross*
   (Tyndale Press).
Morris, Leon. *The Lord from Heaven* (IVP).
Thomas, W.H. Griffith. *Christianity is Christ* (Church
   Book Room Press).

V.   THE HOLY SPIRIT AND CHRISTIAN
   LIVING

Griffiths, M.C. *Consistent Christianity* (IVP).
Hallesby, O. *Prayer* (IVP).
Lloyd-Jones, D.M. *Studies in the Sermon on the
   Mount* (IVP. 2 vols.).
Morris, Leon. *Spirit of the Living God* (IVP).
Murray, John. *Principles of Conduct* (Tyndale Press).
Prior, K.F.W. *The Way of Holiness* (IVP).
Ryle, J.C. *Holiness* (James Clarke).
Ryle, J.C. *Practical Religion* (James Clarke).
Smeaton, G. *The Doctrine of the Holy Spirit* (Banner
   of Truth).

VI.   THE SECOND ADVENT

Grier, W.J. *The Momentous Event* (Evangelical
   Bookshop, Belfast).
Manley, G.T. *The Return of Jesus Christ* (IVP).

VII.   THE CHURCH

Renwick, A.M. *The Story of the Church* (IVP).
Stibbs, A.M. *God's Church* (IVP).